Childhood

in pictures

Pictures
to share

for Jenny and Doug
who loved us.

**Pictures
to share**

First published in 2006 by
Pictures to Share Community Interest Company,
a UK based social enterprise that publishes
illustrated books for older people.

www.picturestoshare.co.uk

ISBN 10 0-9553940-0-7
ISBN 13 978-0-9553940-0-3

Front Cover: Boy running on beach by Frans Jansen. The Image Bank/Getty Images
Endpapers: Daisy chain © Ann Bridges. www.ann-bridges.com
Title page: Baby boy by Kathleen Hanzel. Photographer's Choice/Getty Images
Back cover: Detail from Sympathy by Briton Riviere
Detail from Goldfish bowl by H Armstrong Roberts
Detail from Child hugging snowman by WPh

Childhood

in pictures

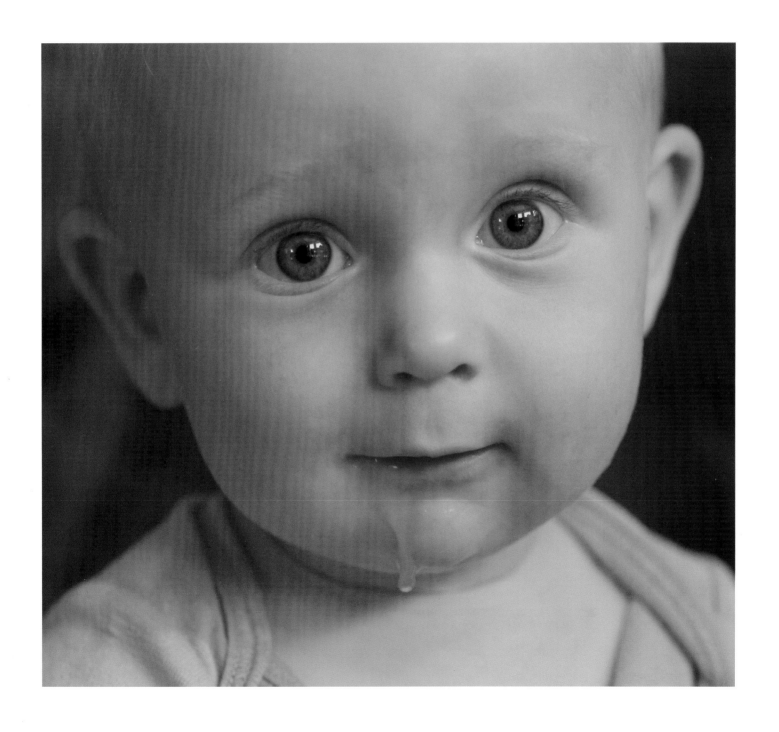

Edited by Helen J Bate

Up and down the country,
Everywhere you'll spy
Little boys, all waiting
To see the trains go by.

What to do this morning?
Hear them all reply:
Let's wait about the station
And see the trains go by.

Quotation: from 'Watching for Trains' by Eleanor Halsey,
from The Youngest Omnibus, Thomas Nelson & Sons 1947.
Main photograph: The Early Bird. Camerique/Archive Photos/
Hulton Archive/Getty Images
Small photograph: Train by Harry Todd. Hulton Archive/Getty Images

Life, within doors,

has few pleasanter prospects than a neatly arranged and well-provisioned breakfast-table.

Quotation from 'The House of the Seven Gables'
by Nathaniel Hawthorn (1804-64)
Illustration: Winter Breakfast by Cicely Mary Barker (1895-1973)
from 'Rhymes New and Old ' published by Blackie and Son.
The Art Archive/Bodleian Library, Oxford, (Shelf No. 25210 d.849.16)

There comes a time

in every boy's life
when he has a raging desire
to go somewhere
and dig for hidden treasure.

Quotation from 'The Adventures of Tom Sawyer' 1876
by Mark Twain (1835-1910)
Photographs: Sunshine Service by Carl Sutton.
Hulton Archive/Getty Images

There is no friend like a sister

In calm or stormy weather;
To cheer one on the tedious way,
To fetch one if one goes astray,
To lift one if one totters down,
To strengthen whilst one stands.

Quotation from 'Goblin Market and other poems' 1862
by Christina Georgina Rossetti (1830-94)
Painting: Children on the Seashore by Dorothea Sharp (1874-1955)
Private Collection/© Whitford & Hughes, London/
The Bridgeman Art Library

If you were poor fifty years ago,

it meant you didn't have enough to eat.

If you're poor now,

it means you only have one car.

Quotation: Sir George Martin (1926 -)
Photographs: Boys on go-cart by Tony Boxall.
Mary Evans Picture Library

In December 1962

a blizzard across south-west England and Wales left drifts six metres deep which blocked roads and rail routes, left villages cut off and brought down power lines. Thanks to further falls and almost continual near-freezing temperatures, snow was still deep on the ground across much of the country three months later.

January 1963

was the month when even the sea froze, the Thames froze right across in places, and ice floes appeared on the river at Tower Bridge.

Everywhere birds literally dropped off their perches, killed by the cold.

Text: from www.metoffice.com
Photograph: Child hugging snowman by WPh. LOOK/Getty Images

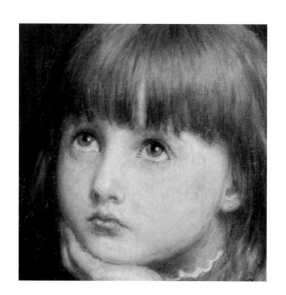

I am so
bored
with it all.

Quotation: Attributed last words of Sir Winston Churchill
Painting: Sympathy by Briton Riviere (1840-1920).
The Bridgeman Art Library/Getty images

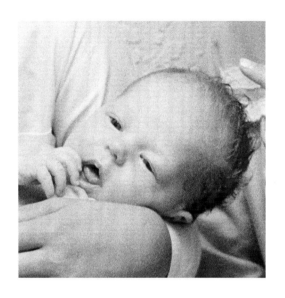

Monday's child
is fair of face,

Tuesday's child
is full of grace,

Wednesday's child
is full of woe,

Thursday's child
has far to go,

Friday's child
is loving and giving,

Saturday's child
works hard for a living,

But the child that is born on the Sabbath day
Is bonny and blithe, and good and gay.

Text: Traditional Rhyme

Photographs: Brother and sisters by H. Armstrong Roberts
Retrofile/Getty Images

The only way to have a friend is to be one.

Main photograph: Two girls by Benn Mitchell
Photographer's Choice/Getty Images
Small photograph: Two children by Barbara Peacock
Taxi/Getty Images

I never lost a little fish.
Yes, I am free to say.
It always was the

biggest fish

I caught that got away.

Quotation: Attributed to Eugene Field (1850-95)
Main photograph: What's the Catch by Harry Todd.
Hulton Archive/Getty Images
Small photograph: Goldfish bowl by H Armstrong Roberts.
Retrofile/Getty Images

The general idea,

of course,
in any first-class laundry
is to see
that no shirt or collar
ever comes back twice.

Quotation from 'Winnowed Wisdom' by Stephen Leacock (1869-1944)
Painting: This is the Way We Wash Our Clothes
by George Dunlop Leslie (1835-1921)
Lady Lever Art Gallery, National Museums Liverpool.

The dog
was created especially for children.

Quotation: Henry Ward Beecher (1813-87)
Photographs: Gypsy boy with dog by Tony Boxall.
Mary Evans Picture Library

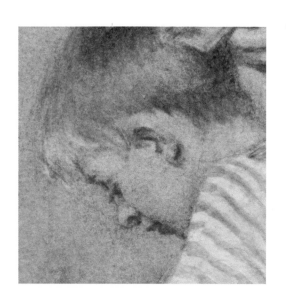

Short
back and sides

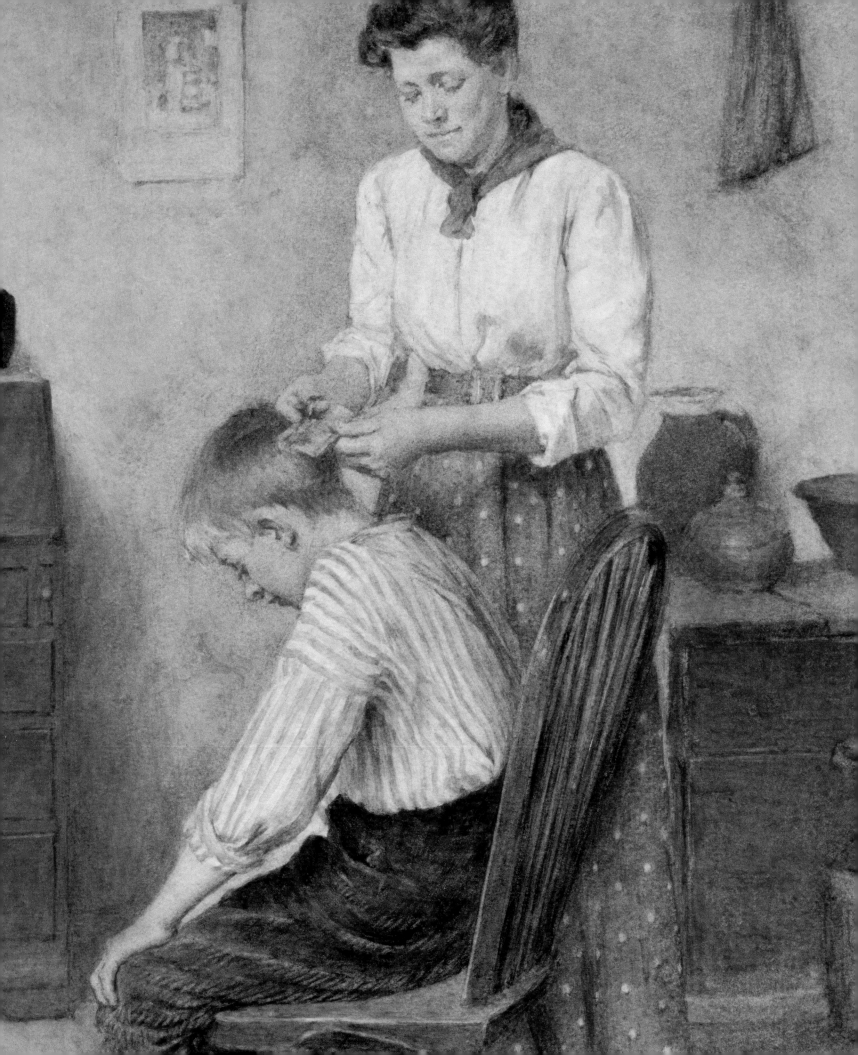

The baby over the way,

I know
Is a better baby than me;
For the baby over the way is all
That a baby ought to be.

The baby over the way is neat,
When I'm not fit to be seen;
His frock is smooth and his bib is sweet,
And his ears are always clean.

He's wide awake when he's put to bed,
But he never screams or cries;
He lies as still as a mouse, 'tis said,
And closes his beautiful eyes.

He's a dear little, sweet little angel bright,
A love and a dove, they say;
**But when I grow up,
I'm going to fight**
With the baby over the way.

Quotation from The Baby Over the Way by Fay Inchfawn
Photographs: Sleeping baby with teddy bear by Tim Platt.
The Image Bank/Getty Images

**Pictures
to share**

Acknowledgements
Our thanks to the many contributors who have allowed their
text or imagery to be used for a reduced or no fee.
Thanks also to all those who assisted in the development of this
book by helping with or taking part in trials; especially Sally Reid,
Occupational Therapist, of Prospect House Nursing Home,
Malpas, and John Thompson, Activities Co-ordinator
at Crawfords Walk Nursing Home, Chester.

All effort has been made to contact copyright holders.
If you own the copyright for work that is represented, but have
not been contacted, please get in touch via our website.

Thanks to our sponsors
The UnLtd Millennium Awards Scheme
The LankellyChase Foundation
The Rayne Foundation
The Cheshire Partnership
Cheshire and Warrington Social Enterprise Partnership

Some quotations have been provided by
'Chambers Dictionary of Quotations',
Chambers Harrap Publishers Ltd, 2005

Published by
Pictures to Share Community Interest Company.
Peckforton, Cheshire
www.picturestoshare.co.uk

Printed in England by
Burlington Press, 1 Station Road, Foxton CB2 6SW